MW01048269

Macklemore

young
reader's
library of pop
biographies

Adele

Katy Perry

Lady Gaga

Macklemore

Nicki Minaj

young
reader's
library of pop
biographies

Macklemore

C. F. Earl

VILLAGE EARTH PRESS

**Young Reader's Library of Pop Biographies:
Macklemore**

Village Earth Press
Vestal, New York 13850
www.villageearthpress.com

First Printing
9 8 7 6 5 4 3 2 1

Series ISBN: 978-1-62524-092-7
ISBN: 978-1-62524-096-5
ebook ISBN: 978-1-62524-145-0
    Library of Congress Control Number: 2014933852

Author: Earl, C. F.

Table of Contents

Chapter One

On Top, Looking Back

Superstar music producer Pharrell Williams was about to announce the winner of the Best New Artist award at the 2014 Grammy Award Show. New music stars like rapper Kendrick Lamar and country singer Kacey Musgraves were up for the award. So were rapper Macklemore and music maker Ryan Lewis. In 2013, Macklemore and Lewis had taken over the music world. Their songs—from the bouncy "Thrift Shop" to the emotional "Same Love"—were playing everywhere.

Macklemore sat in a green suit and bow tie, waiting to hear what Pharrell would say. Ryan Lewis sat to his left.

"And the Grammy goes to. . ." Pharrell tore the envelope slowly. The room felt tense as the audience all held their breath.

"Macklemore and Ryan Lewis!"

Macklemore and Ryan were overcome. They took a second to collect themselves before standing to accept their award. After smiles and congratulations, they walked to the stage.

Macklemore hugged Pharrell and took his Grammy. Macklemore had been chosen as the best new musical artist of 2013.

"Wow, we're here on this stage right now," Macklemore started. "First . . . I want to thank our fans, the people that got us on this stage. . . . Before there was a story, there was our fans and it spread . . . through them. . . . Without them there would be no us."

Macklemore thanked his parents and fiancé before leaving the stage. But he also had another important message.

"We made this album without a **record label**," he told the Grammy audience. While many other artists need record labels to pay for recording, get the music in stores, and advertise the music, Macklemore is **independent**. He does all the work of a record label on his own with the help of a few others, including Ryan Lewis.

In a few years, Macklemore went from rapping for a few serious fans to having a worldwide audience. His album *The Heist* has sold millions of copies and his songs with music partner Ryan Lewis have become major hits. Macklemore is now one of the biggest stars in pop music, with millions of views on YouTube and songs played on every radio station. But one of the most amazing things about Macklemore's story is that he's done all this without the help of a big record label.

A **record label** is a company that publishes and sells music to customers.

Independent means not published by a major record label.

Music History: The Grammy Awards

No award in the music world is more important than the Grammys. For more than fifty years, the Grammys have given people who make music and work in the music business a chance to vote on the best music of the year. The Recording Academy started the Grammys in 1959, and since then, new types of music have been honored with the award—including hip-hop. The first hip-hop Grammy was awarded to The Fresh Prince (actor Will Smith) and DJ Jazzy Jeff in 1989. Hip-hop has been a big part of the Grammy Awards show since then, from Eminem to Kanye West to Macklemore. For more information about the Grammy Awards, including the past winners, visit www.grammy.com.

Macklemore's Grammy win for Best New Artist was just proof of how far the Seattle rapper had come on his own in a short time.

EARLY LIFE

Macklemore wasn't always the superstar rapper that fans know today. Before he was a famous rapper with a hit album, Macklemore was Ben Haggerty, a boy growing up listening to hip-hop in Seattle.

Ben was born on June 19, 1983, in Seattle, Washington. He grew up in a part of Seattle called Capitol Hill. Ben's parents weren't big music fans, but from an early age, Ben loved music more than anything. And he loved hip-hop and rap music more

Macklemore grew up in a town near Seattle, Washington. As a kid, he'd travel into the city to see hip-hop concerts.

than any other kind. Macklemore told television show *106 & Park* that hip-hop was the first music he listened to as a young kid.

"It was the first music that caught my attention," he told host Bow Wow. "I fell in love shortly after."

As a kid, Macklemore had listened to rap group Digital Underground. "That was when I fell in love with it," he said. "That was the music that I always listened to ever since then."

Hip-hop was a big part of Macklemore's adolescence. He remembers listening to it with his friends. "It was the summertime, and we used to make homemade tents," he said in an interview with website HardKnock.tv. "We'd bring the boombox out and listen in the shade in these homemade tents for hours, until we drained the batteries."

Macklemore said he often recorded songs from the radio because he couldn't always buy the music he loved; his parents wouldn't let him buy hip-hop that had swear words in the lyrics—music marked with the Parental Advisory sticker. Besides, he couldn't always afford the music he wanted to hear. So Ben and his friends listened to music on the radio and shared tapes they made themselves. They also went to concerts in Seattle. Hip-hop was Ben's world when he was young.

STARTING IN MUSIC

Ben's love of hip-hop only grew stronger as he got older. Soon, he began doing more than listening. He started performing and making music of his own.

"I started rapping in talent shows . . . trying to be like Michael Jackson," Macklemore told *106 & Park*. "About fourteen years old, [I] started picking up the pen and writing."

As Ben grew up, he listened to all types of hip-hop. He

Today, Macklemore has become a hip-hop star, performing for thousands of fans at each concert. But not too long ago, Macklemore was a fan just like all the people who love his music today.

listened to artists like Nas, Talib Kweli, and the Wu-Tang Clan. He also listened to many lesser-known artists. These artists gave Ben the confidence to start creating his own hip-hop music. Before long, he was writing and recording his own raps, working to be as good as the artists he loved. At the time, Ben was rapping under the name Professor Macklemore.

In 2000, when Ben was still in high school, he recorded an album as Professor Macklemore. He called the group of songs *Open Your Eyes*. The eighteen-song album showed Ben's talent for rap, even though he was still young.

Soon, he'd take his skill for writing and his love of music a lot farther. Ben was a hip-hop fan—but soon he'd be a rap star like the artists he loved to listen to on the radio.

Find Out Even More

When you're looking for information about music, finding books at the library is a great place to start. Try checking your school library for books about the music you love. At the library, you can find books by checking the computer catalog or by asking a librarian for help. Try finding some of these books or other books about music stars or hip-hop:

Brown, Terrell. *Pharrell Williams (Hip Hop)*. Broomall, Penn.: Mason Crest Publishers, 2007.

Hatch, Thomas. *A History of Hip-Hop: The Roots of Rap*. Mankato, Minn.: Capstone Press, 2005.

Llanas, Sheila Griffin. *Hip-Hop Stars (Hip-Hop World)*. Mankato, Minn.: Capstone Press, 2010.

Take a look at the books you've found. Look at the table of contents. Turn to a chapter that you think seems interesting and check out a few pages. As you're reading through the pages of the books, ask yourself the following questions:

1. How is the information in the book organized? Can you find the information you're looking for easily?

Can you use the table of contents and index to find the facts you want to know more about?

2. How well can you understand the information in the book? Finding a book that you can read and understand is an important part of learning more about the topics you love. Different books are written for different readers.

3. Does the book have pictures? How do they help you understand more about the book's topic? If the book has captions, how do they help you learn more about the pictures?

4. Do you like the book? Do you want to read more after taking a quick look? Is there information in this book you can't find in another book?

Chapter Two

Starting Out in Seattle

In the early 2000s, Ben was making music and rapping for small audiences in Seattle. Though he was still young, he was already making his way toward living his dreams. His talent and love of music would take him far—but first, Ben would hit a low point. Though it seemed as though he was set for stardom, drugs soon became a big problem.

HITTING THE BOTTOM ON THE WAY TO THE TOP

Macklemore continued creating music and rapping after high school. A few years after he graduated, he was becoming a successful artist in Seattle. He had fans and performed shows around the city.

Ben was taking classes at Evergreen State College while working to make his music dreams happen. During his time at college, Ben also started working with young people in prison. He taught students at the Green Hill School about music. Green Hill

Ben went to Evergreen State College after high school, but working with young people outside the college campus inspired him even more.

is a school juvenile correctional institution, for people too young for an adult prison.

Macklemore talked with the news website Seattleite.com about how much working with students at the Green Hill School meant to him. "Green Hill is where . . . the 'worst of the worst' type of kids lived. However, it's completely not that—they were incredible kids who just got caught up in other things," he said. "It was an intense experience and it gave me a lot to reflect on in my life."

In 2005, Macklemore put out another album. He called the collection of songs *The Language of My World*. By the time he went to college, Ben had stopped using the name "Professor Macklemore" and shortened it to "Macklemore." The album was his first under his new name, a name he'd make famous in just a few years.

But as Ben was making his way toward his goals, he was also dealing with a growing problem. He was becoming addicted to **prescription painkillers**. Though he was on his way to living his dream, Macklemore had to change his life before he could become the star he is today.

In a documentary about Macklemore and Ryan Lewis made by filmmaker Jabari Johnson, Macklemore talked about his problem with drugs. "I've always struggled with being balanced," he said. ". . . I'm an addict. . . . It's always been this all-or-nothing type of thing."

Drugs were keeping him from reaching

Prescription painkillers are powerful drugs that help people deal with pain, which are so strong that normally you need a doctor's permission to use them.

Ryan Lewis has worked with Macklemore on some of the rapper's biggest songs.

his dreams in music, but they were also damaging his body and mind. Ben would stay inside for days, cutting himself off from friends and family.

In 2008, Ben was fed up with what his life had become. To help himself, he went to a rehabilitation clinic. He changed his life and stopped using drugs. He chose to focus even more on his music and become Macklemore full-time. He wouldn't let drugs stop him from becoming the star he knew he could be.

WORKING WITH RYAN LEWIS

While Macklemore was still having a hard time with drugs, he met Ryan Lewis. Ryan found Macklemore's music on the Internet, and the two got in touch online. They became friends. Ryan and Macklemore worked on some music together, but Ryan mostly worked as a photographer. He took pictures of Macklemore to help him get the word out about his music. After Macklemore stopped using drugs, however, he and Ryan began making music together more. Ryan made beats, and Macklemore focused on writing his rhymes.

In 2009, Macklemore put out another collection of songs, the first since he stopped using drugs. *The Unplanned Mixtape* was released online near the end of 2009. The free album featured some music he'd made with Ryan, along with music from other **producers**.

The Unplanned Mixtape helped Macklemore become more popular

In hip-hop, **producers** make the beats rappers rhyme over, creating new music themselves or using bits of older music.

Macklemore and Ryan put the first music they worked on together on the Internet so fans could listen for free.

outside Seattle. Many new fans were discovering Macklemore's music. The song "And We Danced" became a hit online with help from a funny video. Macklemore would soon become famous for his videos.

Macklemore and Ryan recorded more music together after *The Unplanned Mixtape*. Before long, the pair decided to work with each other and no one else. They began recording a group

Music History: Rap and the Internet

Today, the Internet is a huge part of hip-hop. The Internet is a great way for fans to find new music and new artists to share their songs. Websites follow the latest news and post new music or videos. Listeners can download free mixtapes from their favorite rappers and new artists they've never heard before. Artists like Kendrick Lamar, Drake, and Nicki Minaj have all become stars by first sharing their music on the Internet.

Macklemore has also used the Internet to gain fans around the world. He's posted free music online and put a lot of work into videos that fans will enjoy. The Internet has given artists like Macklemore a way to reach people wherever they live. In the past, an artist from Seattle might never be heard by a hip-hop fan in New York. Today, the Internet brings hip-hop fans together around the music they love—no matter where they are.

of songs they called *The VS. EP*. They released the music online for free, just as Macklemore had put out *The Unplanned Mixtape*. *The VS. EP* helped to make Macklemore even more popular. And fans loved Ryan's beats.

Soon, fans were sharing their music and watching their videos on YouTube. They wanted more music from Macklemore and Ryan. The two had already started making popular music together, but now they'd go on to make some huge hip-hop hits.

Find Out Even More

Reading books is one of the best ways to find out more about the music and artists you love. But one book can never hold all the information you want to know about its subject. A book only has so many pages. The book's author had to choose what to put into the book, as well as what to leave out. Many facts and stories may be left out of the book—not because they aren't important, but because there isn't room to fit in everything. To get a better view of a subject, you'll always want to read more than one book. You can also search the Internet to find out more about almost any topic you're interested in.

Using search engines helps to narrow down all the information online. Search engines like Google, Bing, or Yahoo! find websites based on keywords you choose. Type a few words into the search bar and you can find almost any information you want. But choose your keywords carefully—even a misspelling can bring you websites that have nothing to do with what you're searching for. Here's an example:

Say you want to learn more about Ryan Lewis. So you go to Google and you type in his name—but by mistake you spell his last name "Louis." What comes up when you click the search button? Probably not much about Ryan Lewis—but a lot about people named Ryan Louis.

Now say you want to learn more about how to get

started as a hip-hop artist. So this time you type "hip-hop" and click. The first site you'll see is the Wikipedia page for hip-hop. This might be a pretty good place to start, since Wikipedia offers a good overview on many topics, with links to other sites where you can learn more. But the Wikipedia page is a pretty long one, and when you look at it, you may feel overwhelmed. When you look at the other sites Google offers you, you'll feel even more overwhelmed! There are just too many sites—and none of them look like what you want.

Here's the trick: you need to narrow down your search as much as possible. Try phrases like "starting out in hip-hop," "rap beginner," and "learn to rap." This time you'll see what you're looking for. You may need to click on a few sites and skim through them before you find exactly what you're looking for—but you're on the right track now.

Chapter Three

Macklemore's Big Heist

Macklemore and Ryan Lewis had success with songs on *The Unplanned Mixtape* and their *VS. EP*. Sharing their music online and performing their songs had earned them fans around the world. But soon, the pair would take their success to the next level. While other rappers might try to get a record deal, Macklemore and Ryan were focused on making the best music they could. Before long, they would put out one of the most successful hip-hop albums in recent years—and without a record company behind them.

THE HEIST

After *The Unplanned Mixtape*, Macklemore and Ryan released a few new songs in 2011. Just as he had before, Macklemore put their music on the Internet so the most people possible could hear the songs. Fans were glad to have new music from the Seattle rapper on his way to the top.

First, Macklemore and Ryan put out a song called "Wing$" in January. The song is about Macklemore's love for shoes, and basketball shoes most of all. The song isn't just about buying fancy sneakers, though. Like many of Macklemore's songs, "Wing$" is also about much more. Macklemore wrote on his blog that the song is about trying to find happiness and meaning in buying things. The song tells how the happiness you can find through buying something doesn't last.

Later in the year, Macklemore and Ryan put out another song. "Can't Hold Us" hit the Internet in August 2011. Both "Wing$" and "Can't Hold Us" would become huge hits for Macklemore, but it would take time for the songs to become popular. Both songs would be on their next album, *The Heist.*

In July 2012, Macklemore and Ryan put out a video on Ryan's YouTube channel, announcing the date fans could get their hands on new music from the pair. In the video, Macklemore talks about how hard he and his team worked on the album after they'd finished *the VS. EP.* After bringing fans behind the scenes of his life during his time recording his new album, *The Heist,* Macklemore let fans know they could get the album in October 2012.

In the same month, Macklemore released another song that would become a huge hit. "Same Love," like many of Macklemore's most popular songs, has a message. The song talks about the **stereotypes** many people have about gay people. Hip-hop hasn't always been very sympathetic to gay and lesbian issues, but "Same Love" brought the need for **LGBT** equality out into the open. In the song, Macklemore also raps about his uncles, who are gay, and how he feels they should be able to get married if they want to.

A few months before the release of *The Heist*, Macklemore released a song that would become one of his most popular. "Thrift Shop" came out in August 2012. The fun song starts with a catchy saxophone part and toe-tapping beat. Macklemore raps about finding cheap clothes at the thrift shop that other people would never wear and making them cool. His rhymes are funny as he teases hip-hop songs that are all about expensive clothes. Like "Same Love," the message in "Thrift Shop" is different from many other rap songs on the radio. Macklemore's messages helped him stand out and become popular.

Next, Macklemore put out another single. "White Walls" featured Los Angeles rapper Schoolboy Q. Like the other singles from *The Heist*, "White Walls" played on the radio and became a hit. The song wasn't as big as some of the other songs on the album, but it was another reminder of Macklemore's skill at creating catchy songs.

The Heist was a huge success almost immediately. In the first week the album was out, fans bought tens of thousands of copies. The album came in at number two on the *Billboard* album charts in its first week, selling more than almost any other album that week.

Macklemore performed on the *Ellen* talk show in October and gained many more fans. Ellen DeGeneres

Stereotypes are oversimplified ideas people have about a certain group, without a good reason.

LGBT stands for lesbian, gay, bisexual, and transgender people.

With hits like "Thrift Shop," "Same Love," and "Can't Hold Us," Macklemore was quickly becoming one of hip-hop's most exciting rising stars.

introduced him and Ryan as her "heroes" for the way they had spoken out in their song "Same Love."

The more people heard Macklemore's music on television shows like *Ellen*, the more people bought his music. Songs like "Thrift Shop," "Same Love," and "Can't Hold Us" played on radio stations throughout the United States. Macklemore's music became even more popular in 2013. His album kept selling and people kept watching his videos on YouTube.

Macklemore's videos were exciting. In the video for "Can't Hold Us," he raps on a pirate ship. In "Thrift Shop," Macklemore wears different costumes, including pajamas. The video

Music History: The *Billboard* Charts

In 1894, *Billboard* magazine was started to give readers information about entertainment they could see performed. Years later, *Billboard* began to focus on music. By the 1940s, the magazine was known for keeping track of the most popular music, making charts to show which songs sold the most. Since then, reaching the top of the *Billboard* song or album charts have been a sign of success for artists making every kind of music.

for "Same Love" is a bit different. The emotional video shows different couples falling in love and getting married.

At the beginning of 2013, "Thrift Shop" became a number-one hit on the *Billboard* Hot 100 song chart. Soon, "Can't Hold Us" also became a number-one song. "Same Love" reached number eleven on the same chart as well. By April, *The Heist* had sold more than half a million copies. By the end of 2013, more than one million fans bought the album, and Macklemore's videos had been watched hundreds of millions of times on the Internet.

Macklemore had grown up listening to amazing hip-hop albums by the artists he loved. Now, he had made his own hip-hop **classic**, with the hit songs and sales numbers to prove it.

Something that is **classic** is recognized by almost everyone as being so well-made and important that it will last a long time.

After the release of *The Heist*, Macklemore hit the road to perform his songs for fans outside the United States.

MACKLEMORE TOURS THE WORLD

After the success of *The Heist*, Macklemore and Ryan started a tour to perform their music for fans around the world. Between August and December, Macklemore and Ryan performed in Germany, England, France, and the United States.

For many concerts on the world tour, rappers Big K.R.I.T. and Talib Kweli opened the show. Macklemore had grown up listening to Talib Kweli—and now he was on tour with one of his idols.

Macklemore and Ryan made videos about their tour and put them out on the Internet. The video series showed Macklemore performing and life behind the scenes on tour. Just as Macklemore had shared his music online, tour videos let a huge number of people see what a Macklemore concert might look like without having to pay a cent. Fans who couldn't see the tour got a taste of Macklemore's performances, and fans who did go got to see a bit more than the show.

Macklemore and Ryan had amazing success with their first album together. They'd had hit songs on the radio and sold more than a million copies of *The Heist*. The two had toured the world and performed for thousands of fans. Macklemore had come a long way from rapping to a few dozen fans in Seattle clubs. Soon, he'd perform for the biggest audience of his music career.

Find Out Even More

If you go to Google.com and try searching for "Macklemore," you'll find millions of results. Take a look at the list below to see just a few of the many websites you can find on the Seattle rapper.

Macklemore & Ryan Lewis
macklemore.com
Macklemore - Wikipedia, the free encyclopedia
en.wikipedia.org/wiki/Macklemore
Macklemore (macklemore) on Twitter
twitter.com/macklemore
Macklemore & Ryan Lewis | New Music And Songs | MTV
www.mtv.com/artists/macklemore-and-ryan-lewis
Macklemore | Facebook
www.facebook.com/Macklemore
Macklemore's Profile • Instagram
instagram.com/macklemore

Search engines will bring you millions of websites about Macklemore. But not every site is a good source of information about his music or his life. Which of the sites listed is the best place to find facts about Macklemore?

Don't just start at the top of the list Google gives and work your way down. Just because a site is a the top doesn't mean it's necessarily the *best* site. Macklemore.com is the official site for Macklemore and Ryan Lewis. The site was created by Macklemore and Ryan to share information about new music or concerts. It's probably the best source of information about Macklemore and his music that you can find on the Internet. Official sites are almost always the first place you should look for information on an artist you like.

Wikipedia can be a good source of information about music and other topics. But always be careful to check the sources in Wikipedia articles you read. To find the source of the information posted on Wikipedia, click the small number near a fact you want to check. You should be able to find the website where that fact was first posted. Remember that anyone can post information on Wikipedia, and that information doesn't usually come from the artists themselves. Checking the facts on Wikipedia is the best way to be sure information you're reading is true.

Social media can be a great way to find out new information straight from the artists themselves. But always be sure that you're hearing from the artist by checking to see if the Twitter, Facebook, or Instagram account is official. On Twitter, for example, you can search for the blue check to make sure you're hearing from Macklemore and not a fan pretending to be him. The blue check means that Twitter has "verified" the account and you can be sure it's really Macklemore.

Be patient. The Internet is a great source for information, but it can take some time to sort through all the information it offers to find exactly what you're looking for.

Chapter Four

Macklemore Today

Macklemore and Ryan Lewis had climbed to the top of the music world. In late 2013, the two were rewarded for all their hard work with a group of Grammy **nominations**. When the 2014 Grammy nominations were announced near the end of the year, Macklemore talked to MTV about how happy he was to be nominated.

"I never thought that our music would affect this many people and be heard by this many people," he said. "So it's the highest honor; it's the peak of what you strive for in terms of being recognized for the music that you made, and it's just exciting."

Macklemore wasn't just nominated for Grammys; he was also asked to perform at the award show ceremony. He would be

Nominations are when you are considered to win an award. You might not win, but you're in the running.

performing in front of an audience of millions on live television. Fans who had been listening to Macklemore for years were thrilled when the news came out that he'd be performing at the awards show. Their favorite Seattle rapper had come a long way.

MACKLEMORE'S BIG NIGHT AT THE GRAMMYS

On the night of the Grammy Award show, things couldn't have gone much better for Macklemore and Ryan. The two were nominated for seven awards. Before the show, they got news that they'd won three awards already. "Thrift Shop" won the awards for Best Rap Song and Best Rap Performance. *The Heist* also won in the Best Rap Album category, beating albums from stars like Kanye West and Jay-Z.

During the awards show, Macklemore and Ryan also won the Best New Artist award and thanked their fans on stage. They had won four Grammys in just one year, more than many artists win in their entire careers. But the biggest part of Macklemore's night came later on in the show.

Near the end of the Grammy award show, rapper and actor Queen Latifah took the stage to introduce Macklemore and Ryan. She talked about the importance of love and letting gays and lesbians who love people of the same sex get married just as straight people can. Queen Latifah also announced that during the performance of the smash hit "Same Love," thirty-four couples would be getting married—including some same-sex couples—right there in the theater.

Macklemore and Ryan performed their hit song in front of millions of television viewers. Near the end of the song, the pair had another surprise, too. Pop superstar Madonna came on stage to perform with singer Mary Lambert, Macklemore, and Ryan. As the song came to a close, the couples getting married kissed and cried, happy to be married. The crowd at the show cheered for the new couples.

The Grammy performance was a huge moment for Macklemore and Ryan. They had reached the very top of the music world by making music with big, important messages. Now, they had won awards for their meaningful songs and successful album.

CHANGING THE MUSIC BUSINESS

Macklemore and Ryan have had amazing success musically. But they've also done amazing things in the business of music. Without a big record company behind them, Macklemore and Ryan have become one of the most successful acts in music.

Instead of having a company pay for recording, t-shirts, or concerts, Macklemore and Ryan pay for everything themselves. They have created their own business. The two of them have put together a team of people to sell clothes, concert tickets, music, and more.

Macklemore and Ryan are independent artists. That means they work for themselves. Because they pay for everything themselves, they don't have a big company taking any of the money they make. That means they get to keep more money than many artists who work with bigger companies.

Macklemore and Ryan can decide how the money their music makes gets spent. They choose to put a lot of what they make back into recording more music or making a better live show. Because they're independent, they can make that decision. They don't have to ask to put out new music or print a new t-shirt.

Instead, they control everything themselves, with help from their friends.

Macklemore and Ryan aren't just great at making music. They're smart businesspeople who understand how to make money with their art. They get to control their own path in the music world and make all their own decisions. It can be difficult to run your own business in music. But Macklemore and Ryan have proven that you don't need a record company to become successful.

MACKLEMORE'S PERSONAL LIFE

Macklemore has done amazing things in music and business. But he's also grown up a lot since he was rapping in Seattle and having problems with drugs. Macklemore talked to filmmaker Jabari Johnson about changing his life for the better over time. "I've felt so many times what it's like to feel failure . . . what it's like to let people who love you down," Macklemore told Jabari. "I've had so much of my life—particularly in my twenties—spent in that place of trying to fight my way out of that. I don't want to do it anymore. I want to be somebody that is respected, and not just for my music. I want to be respected in terms of the way I treat people."

When someone who is addicted to drugs has **relapsed**, it means he has used them again after a period of being clean.

Macklemore admits he isn't perfect. He knows that addiction is still a problem he must always face. He raps about staying away from using drugs. He's also admitted that he **relapsed** in 2011.

Macklemore's Style

Macklemore's catchy songs and smart rhymes have made him a star. But the Seattle rapper's fun sense of style has also been a big part of his success. Style and clothing have always been part of hip-hop, but Macklemore has a way of dressing that is all his own. Just as he talked about in "Thrift Shop," Macklemore loves to wear clothes other people might think are silly or uncool. He's rapped in videos wearing big fur hats. He's worn brightly colored Hawaiian shirts during interviews. He loves bright colors and bold styles. Macklemore is always willing to wear something others might be embarrassed to put on. His style has helped him stand out.

Macklemore's hair has helped him get noticed, as well. He has the sides of his head shaved, with his long, blonde hair slicked back on top. He has said that when he goes out wearing a hat, fewer fans recognize him. Many people may have never heard a Macklemore song, but they know the rapper's hairstyle!

Macklemore says his new fame and money can sometimes make his struggle with drugs harder. Today, Macklemore is working hard to keep himself healthy and on the path to success.

Macklemore also made a big change in his life in early 2013, when he got engaged. On January 21, he asked his long-time girlfriend Tricia Davis to marry him. Macklemore and Tricia have been together for many years. Macklemore told *People Magazine* about the couple's engagement: "We scaled down a mountain. I got down on one knee and told her how much I loved her. It was really beautiful."

Tricia used to work as a nurse, but today she's busy helping Macklemore and Ryan run their business. She works with them on their videos and their style. She also helps Macklemore and Ryan with the clothes they sell and helps them spread the word about their music.

Macklemore has come a long way from the darker times he went through when he was younger. He's worked hard to put drugs behind him and get his life together. Today, he's on top of the music world, and he's working with Tricia. Things couldn't be going much better for the rapper from Seattle.

LOOKING TO THE FUTURE

In just a few years, Macklemore has become one of the most popular rappers in the world. He has earned millions of fans with his smart lyrics and fun songs. With his huge night at the 2014 Grammys and his hit songs, Macklemore has become a star like the rappers he loved listening to as a kid. He's gone from being a fan to being one of hip-hop's biggest performers.

Millions of fans around the world wait to hear what's next from their favorite new rapper. Many wonder whether he'll keep putting out his own music or if he'll work with a record label in the future. Others ask if he'll continue to make music with Ryan Lewis or decide to work with other producers.

The Heist was a huge success, but only time will tell if Macklemore can reach the same heights with his next album. But no matter what Macklemore decides to do next, his fans are sure to be excited.

Find Out Even More

Websites are great places to find information about the things that interest you—and they're also a great way to get information for school reports and other assignments. With the information right there, it seems pretty easy to highlight the parts you want to include in your project, hit copy, and then hit paste into your document. It's so tempting to do that and save yourself the time of writing it all out all over again in your own words!

But there's a word for that. It's called plagiarism. It's kind of like stealing. You're taking someone else's words and claiming them as yours. It's definitely not the right way to write a report!

Lots of information is freely available on the Internet—but that doesn't mean you're free to take it and claim it as your own. It's okay to quote some sentences or even a paragraph or two from someone's site, but be sure you give credit to the person or organization that wrote the words that you're including. Put quotation marks around the part you're quoting, so people will be able to see that those words were first said or written by someone else.

Here's What We Recommend

IN BOOKS

Anniss, Matt. *The Story of Hip-Hop*. Mankato, Minn.: Smart Apple Media, 2013.

Cornish, Melanie J. *The History of Hip-Hop*. New York: Crabtree Publishing Company, 2009.

Garofoli, Wendy. *Hip-Hop History*. Mankato, Minn.: Capstone Press, 2010.

Rockworth, Janice. *Nas*. Broomall, Pa.: Mason Crest Publishers, 2008.

Rockworth, Janice. *Wu-Tang Clan*. Broomall, Pa.: Mason Crest Publishers, 2008.

ONLINE

Macklemore & Ryan Lewis' Official Site
macklemore.com

Macklemore on Twitter
twitter.com/Macklemore

Macklemore & Ryan Lewis on MTV.com
www.mtv.com/artists/macklemore-and-ryan-lewis

Macklemore on Billboard.com
www.billboard.com/artist/1490130/macklemore

Index

About the Author

C.F. Earl is a writer living and working in Binghamton, New York. Earl writes on a range of topics, including pop culture, history, and health.

Picture Credits

6: San Francisco Foghorn
10: Daniel Schwen
12: The Come Up Show
16: The Come Up Show
18: Gregg M. Erickson
20: San Francisco Foghorn

22: San Francisco Foghorn
26: Christopher Dube
30: The Come Up Show
32: The Come Up Show
36: alaina buzas

CPSIA information can be obtained
at www.ICGtesting.com
Printed in the USA
LVOW01*1758100416

482941LV00001B/2/P

9 781625 240965

.